It's Bedtime

Elyse Woellner

Copyright © 2019 by Elyse Woellner

ISBN: Softcover   9781645505860

Illustrated by Frances Espanol

All rights reserved. No part of this book may be reproduced or transmitted in any form or by any means, electronic or mechanical, including photocopying, recording, or by any information storage and retrieval system, without permission in writing from the copyright owner.

This is a work of fiction. Names, characters, places and incidents either are the product of the author's imagination or are used fictitiously, and any resemblance to any actual persons, living or dead, events, or locales is entirely coincidental.

For Lochlan and Harper

Come on, everyone. It's bedtime!

The sun has gone to bed,
so we must too.

Get into bed and snuggle.

Goodnight, Mr. Moon.

Goodnight, glowing stars.

Goodnight, shiny rain boots.

Goodnight, red helmet.

Goodnight, spiky green dinosaur.

Goodnight, my teddy.

Goodnight, everyone!

www.ingramcontent.com/pod-product-compliance
Lightning Source LLC
Chambersburg PA
CBHW041122070526
44584CB00002B/252